Original title:
Dappled Voices Among the Elf Soft

Author: Sara Säde
ISBN HARDBACK: 978-1-80562-700-5
ISBN PAPERBACK: 978-1-80564-221-3

Elusive Hums from the Starry Glade

In the glade where whispers play,
A tune glimmers, lost by day.
Beneath the gaze of twinkling stars,
Secret songs from worlds afar.

Mossy carpets cushion feet,
Where shadows and moonlight meet.
Elusive hums fill the night air,
With magic swirling everywhere.

Branches sway, a silent dance,
Enthralling all in their trance.
Each note a thread of ancient lore,
Drawing dreamers to explore.

The fireflies join in the tune,
Dancing below a silvery moon.
As laughter weaves through calm and peace,
A night of wonder that won't cease.

Hearts entwined with the melody,
In the glade, wild and free.
With every hum, a wish takes flight,
Lost dreams beckoned by the night.

Mirth in the Celestial Dewdrops

In dawn's embrace, soft and bright,
Dewdrops sparkle with sheer delight.
Each pearl of water tells a tale,
Of cosmic joy that cannot pale.

Beneath the boughs of ancient trees,
Laughter flutters on the breeze.
A symphony of glee and cheer,
As nature's whispers draw you near.

Sunlight dances on emerald grass,
In every corner, wonders amass.
Here, the mundane fades away,
In mirth where dreams and spirits play.

Butterflies join the joyous spree,
Spreading laughter wild and free.
Each droplet shines with newfound glow,
As magic blooms, a radiant show.

With every step, a spark ignites,
Connecting hearts on these bright nights.
In the dewdrops, love is spun,
Mirth that twinkles, never done.

Medley of Echoing Laughter at the Dusk

As dusk enfolds the world in grace,
A medley starts, a merry chase.
Laughter echoes through the trees,
Carried high on the evening breeze.

Soft shadows fall, a gentle tide,
Where enchantment and joy reside.
With every giggle that entwines,
The air ignites with spark divine.

Gathered friends, in circles round,
With tales and jests, a joyful sound.
Each story shared, a thread so bright,
Woven deep into the night.

Stars awaken, twinkling smiles,
Gilding laughter across the miles.
With every note, spirits soar high,
Painting the canvas of the sky.

As the moon dances, silver and bright,
Still the echoes shimmer with light.
A symphony found in every heart,
In the dusk's embrace, we will never part.

Forever bound by joyful dreams,
In laughter's glow, we find our seams.
At twilight's close, let hearts ignite,
In a medley of love under starry night.

Shimmers of Twilight Between the Trees

The sun dips low, a golden thread,
Whispers linger, softly spread.
Leaves dance gently, shadows play,
Twilight breathes a dusky ray.

Moonlight peeks through branches tight,
A hush descends, the coming night.
Creatures stir in hidden glade,
In this realm, no fear, no shade.

Stars awaken, glittering bright,
Guiding spirits, taking flight.
Misty whispers call my name,
In this dance, all souls the same.

Branches sway, the air grows sweet,
Nature's pulse, a heart's retreat.
Here, the day's end softly sings,
Magic glimmers, and freedom brings.

With every step on mossy ground,
The essence of the dusk is found.
Coal-black shadows, silver beams,
In the twilight, we weave our dreams.

Songs of the Twilight Fae

In glimmers soft, the fae do sing,
With voices light as butterfly wing.
They weave their tales in threads of air,
In the twilight's magic, free from care.

Delicate laughter twirls and swirls,
In moonlit pools, the magic unfurls.
Wings made of gossamer and dew,
Each note echoes, sweet and true.

Hidden beneath the ancient trees,
Their songs drift lightly on the breeze.
A world awakened from the day,
When starlight guides the fae's own way.

Gathered in circles, a shimmering band,
With flickering lights, they take a stand.
Dancing 'neath the crescent's glow,
In the heart of night, their secrets flow.

Whispers of hope in harmony rise,
As starlit dreams touch the skies.
In twilight's kiss, the magic sways,
In the fae's realm, forever stays.

Reflections of Magic in the Ferns

In emerald fronds, the magic weaves,
A silent pact, the earth believes.
Sunlight dapples with gentle grace,
In every glimmer, a hidden place.

Ripples of wonder in the stream,
Ferns bow low in a waking dream.
Each tender leaf holds stories old,
Of brave hearts and treasures untold.

Beneath the canopies of green,
The whispers of the past are seen.
Footsteps soft on nature's floor,
Each moment, a glimpse of lore.

The forest breathes, a living heart,
In its embrace, we're never apart.
Reflections mirror the soul's own light,
In every fern, there shines a night.

Here in shadows, secrets hide,
With every glance, the world's tied.
An endless dance of life, reclaimed,
In the fern's realm, wonder is named.

Enchantment in the Meadow's Breath

Beneath the sky, where daisies sway,
In meadows bright, magic finds its way.
Whispers of breeze through golden grass,
Each moment held, like hours pass.

Butterflies flit with tints ablaze,
In every flutter, the sunlight plays.
Petals open, a fragrant hum,
In this realm, the quiet comes.

The scent of earth, the blooms in bloom,
Nature's soft brush dispels the gloom.
An orchestra of buzzing sound,
Where joy in colors can be found.

Amid the blooms, enchantment lies,
As day softens, the daylight dies.
Stars peek out, and night begins,
A tapestry where magic spins.

In meadow's heart, dreams take their flight,
With every breath, the stars ignite.
In this twilight, together we tread,
In love with the whispers, beautifully wed.

Veils of Light in Whispering Woods

Amidst the trees where shadows play,
A canvas woven of night and day.
Soft whispers drift on the gentle breeze,
As sunlight dances through emerald leaves.

Hidden paths where dreams take flight,
In the heart of woods, the air feels bright.
Veils of light weave tales untold,
In secret glades, and hearts unfold.

Sprigs of magic, in silence they hum,
As ancient spirits twirling come.
Songs of the forest, sweet refrains,
Echo softly through the silvered veins.

Each flicker a promise, each rustle a sign,
In this sacred grove where destinies entwine.
A world beyond what the eye can see,
Where time stands still, and souls fly free.

Sun-kissed moments, forever to keep,
In the whispering woods, where dreams never sleep.

Luminous Reveries of the Woodland Spirits

In twilight's embrace, the spirits gleam,
Waltzing softly in a moonlit dream.
With glimmering eyes and laughter aflame,
They call to the wanderer, whispering names.

Hidden in shadows, their secrets reside,
In luminous reveries, they do confide.
Each glittering leaf a tale to unfold,
Of magic and wonder, rich as spun gold.

Through thickets of ivy, they twine and sway,
Guardians of night, guiding the way.
Each moment alive with an ethereal glow,
As the woodland spirits put on their show.

With each fluttering wing and rustling sound,
The echoes of laughter dance all around.
A festival woven with colors divine,
In the heart of the forest, where dreams intertwine.

So linger a moment, let time slip away,
In luminous realms where the shadows play.

Flickers of Sunbeams on Mossy Paths

Through emerald canopies, sunbeams break,
A mosaic of light on the forest's lake.
Flickers dance gently on mossy paths,
As nature's own brush creates lovely swaths.

With each step taken, the earth holds its breath,
In harmony woven where life meets death.
The whispers of ages, in shadows reside,
Guiding the wanderers, side by side.

Crickets all chorus, a serenade sweet,
In rhythm with heartbeats, their melody fleet.
A tapestry rich, in moments unfurl,
As sunbeams cascade, and shadows whirl.

The scent of fresh earth, the call of the vine,
Each flicker a memory, softly divine.
In this sacred space, where stillness abounds,
Every flicker a story, every whisper resounds.

So wander with wonder, with spirit alight,
Along the mossy paths kissed by daylight.

Harmonies of the Ethereal Beings

In the stillness covered by softest night,
Ethereal beings glow with delight.
Harmonies echo through branches above,
Threads of their magic, woven with love.

With a flick of a wrist, they paint the sky,
Each star a wish, they watch and sigh.
In tones like the breeze, their laughter rings,
A symphony rich, that softly sings.

Through twilight meadows, their melodies float,
In whispers of stories, shared by the mote.
Each note a longing, a dream spun anew,
Of joyous beginnings, and hearts beating true.

The wind carries secrets, the trees hum along,
In the embrace of the night, where spirits belong.
Harmonies weave like threads of a loom,
Creating a tapestry, dispelling the gloom.

So dance with the echoes, let your soul soar,
In this realm where the ethereal explores.

The Language of Gossamer Dreams

In whispers soft as morning mist,
The dreams take flight on gentle air,
They weave a tale of magic's kiss,
A tapestry of hope laid bare.

Through moonlit glades where shadows play,
The echoes dance in silver glows,
With every sigh, they drift away,
In gossamer threads where wonder grows.

A secret language, sweet and rare,
In starlit nights, they softly scheme,
For every heart, they lay a snare,
To capture joy within a dream.

Beneath the stars, time takes its flight,
Each pulse of magic, a heartbeat strong,
Through veils of dusk and dawn's first light,
The language whispers, pure and long.

So listen close, with open soul,
Embrace the dreams that rise and soar,
The gossamer threads will make you whole,
A song of hope forevermore.

Echoes of Enchantment

In forests deep where fairies dwell,
Echoes of laughter drift and twine,
With every sound, a silken spell,
A world of wonder, pure and fine.

The trees, they sway in gentle grace,
Their leaves, a choir of whispered tones,
In nature's heart, we find our place,
Among the magic, we are known.

With twilight wrapped in velvet hue,
The moon bestows a silver glow,
Each fleeting moment, fresh and new,
In echoes soft where dreamers go.

A symphony of night takes flight,
As stars like lanterns start to gleam,
With every twinkle, pure delight,
The night unveils its whispered dream.

So close your eyes, let visions bloom,
Let enchantment dance upon your heart,
For in the dark, dispelling gloom,
Live echoes of magic, never part.

Flickering Chimes of Twilight

As daylight fades, the chimes begin,
A melody of dusk and dawn,
With every note, a tale spins in,
Of fleeting moments now withdrawn.

The skies aglow with blush and sigh,
In hues of tangerine and blue,
They beckon stars from depths on high,
To weave a dance that feels so true.

Faint whispers blow on twilight's breeze,
With secrets spun from dusk till night,
Through branches swaying with such ease,
A symphony that feels just right.

The world transforms in silver lights,
As shadows stretch with gentle grace,
In flickering dreams of starry nights,
Our hearts entwined, we find our place.

So linger long where twilight glows,
With chimes that sing of love and fate,
In every flicker, magic flows,
A timeless dance that will await.

Songs of the Sylvan Grove

In sylvan groves where wild things sing,
A harmony of earth and sky,
With every breeze, the branches swing,
A symphony that won't deny.

The flowers bloom with colors bright,
In whispers soft, they tell their tale,
With petals swaying in pure delight,
Each moment captured, like a sail.

The brook will babble tales of yore,
It carries secrets, laughter's song,
To every creature, it will implore,
The joy of life where we belong.

With gentle hands, the woods embrace,
A warm cocoon of nature's love,
In every nook, we find our grace,
As songs of peace unfold above.

So wander deep in nature's thrall,
Where sylvan dreams and spirits meet,
In every echo, hear the call,
The timeless songs that feel so sweet.

Songs of Luminous Shadows

In the forest where dreams intertwine,
The shadows sway, a dance divine.
Whispers echo, ancient and sweet,
A melody found where silence meets.

Glimmering lights flicker in the night,
Guiding wandering souls with their light.
Softly they sing of forgotten lore,
A promise of magic forevermore.

Amongst the trees, secrets abound,
In every rustle, a story is found.
With every note, a heart will soar,
Bound by the magic we can't ignore.

Through luminous shadows, journeys unfold,
Adventures await, just be bold.
In the embrace of the twilight's glow,
The songs of the night will always flow.

Enchanted Whispers on the Bridge of Leaves

Upon the bridge where the leaves entwine,
Whispers dance in a chorus fine.
Echoes of laughter, light as a breeze,
Woven in dreams beneath ancient trees.

Every step holds a tale untold,
A shimmer of magic in green and gold.
The forest beckons with secrets to share,
As sunlight filters through the air.

In the rustling leaves, you'll hear a sigh,
A symphony sung by the low-flying sky.
The softest murmur, a gentle guide,
On this bridge where mysteries abide.

So linger a moment, breathe in the cheer,
For the enchanted whispers embrace you near.
Hold tight the magic, let it ignite,
The wonders that bloom in the veil of night.

Kaleidoscope of Fairies in Flight

In a garden vast where the wildflowers grow,
A kaleidoscope twirls, a vibrant show.
Fairies shimmer with laughter and light,
Dancing on wind, taking flight.

Their wings paint colors across the blue,
A tapestry woven from morning dew.
Each fluttering shimmer, a wish on its way,
Spreading joy with every sway.

Through the petals, they flit and play,
Chasing the sun as it fades away.
Beneath the moon's watchful, silvery glow,
The magic of night invites them to flow.

With every sparkle, a moment defined,
Reminding us of the wonders we find.
To believe in their grace, a heart must ignite,
In the kaleidoscope's glow, day turns to night.

Folklore Weaved in the Canopy

High in the canopy, legends are spun,
Of brave little creatures and the battles they've won.
With every rustle and crack of a branch,
Old tales awaken, a fantastical dance.

The stories of yore, through time they flow,
With magic and courage, they continue to grow.
Bound by the roots of those who believed,
In the folklore of nature, we are all weaved.

A tapestry vibrant, each thread tells a bliss,
A promise of wonders we can't help but miss.
Listen closely as the nightingale sings,
Of heroes and journeys and the hope that it brings.

In shadows and moonlight, let your spirit fly,
For the folklore we cherish will never die.
It dwells in our hearts, like a soft, gentle breeze,
Whispering stories that put us at ease.

Whispers of the Enchanted Glade

In the heart of twilight's glow,
Where secrets dance and shadows flow,
Whispers weave through ancient trees,
Telling tales upon the breeze.

Butterflies flit on silken air,
Delicate whispers everywhere,
A melody of nature's grace,
In the glade, time slows its pace.

Moonbeams twinkle, soft and bright,
Casting dreams in silver light,
The stars, they wink with knowing eyes,
As magic stirs beneath the skies.

Mossy carpets, rich and deep,
Where woodland creatures gently sleep,
Their dreams entwined with softest sighs,
In magic realms where wonder lies.

So linger here, in twilight's gaze,
Let the whispers set you ablaze,
For in this glade, enchanted, fair,
The heart finds peace in nature's care.

Choreography of Shadows and Light

In the dance of dusk and dawn,
Shadows stretch and then are gone,
Light twirls gently with a sigh,
Painting stories in the sky.

Windswept branches sway and bend,
Nature's rhythm, without end,
Each flicker tells of yesteryears,
Softly laced with laughter's tears.

As the sun dips low and shy,
Echoes of a soft goodbye,
Night unfurls its velvet sheet,
Where shadows and the cosmos meet.

Stars peep in, with playful delight,
Catching whispers of the night,
They waltz in a cosmic show,
As the moon begins to glow.

So come and feel the evening's grace,
In the space where light can trace,
A choreography, bold and true,
Of shadows dancing just for you.

Murmurs in the Mystical Grove

Within the grove, a soft refrain,
Old as time, yet fresh as rain,
Murmurs call from twisted vines,
Ancient wisdom, through the pines.

Silver ferns in moonlight sway,
Guarding secrets of the day,
Each rustle carries stories old,
In soft whispers, truth unfolds.

Crickets chirp their nighttime tune,
Beneath the watchful eye of moon,
The stars, they flicker, join in song,
In the grove, you can't go wrong.

Hushed conversations, soft and clear,
Drunk on magic, year to year,
From every nook, a tale to share,
In this grove, love fills the air.

So wander forth, find your own voice,
In the murmurs, make a choice,
To dwell where nature's heart beats slow,
In the embrace of the mystical grove.

Lullabies Beneath the Ancient Boughs

Underneath the boughs so wide,
Where dreams and nighttime secrets bide,
Lullabies weave through the leaves,
Cradling hearts that nature cleaves.

Branches cradle the stars above,
Whispering tales of timeless love,
Cozy nests in twilight's hue,
Where slumber calls for me and you.

Gentle breezes softly sigh,
As fireflies paint the evening sky,
Each glimmer, a promise to keep,
As the world falls fast asleep.

The owl hoots a lullaby sweet,
Echoes dance on quiet feet,
While shadows lurk in corners tight,
Holding secrets of the night.

So come and rest, let worries cease,
Beneath these boughs, find your peace,
In lullabies that nature sings,
Together, welcome what night brings.

Tidal Rhythms of the Leafy Realm

In whispers soft, the leaves do sway,
Their verdant dance, a grand ballet.
Each gust a pulse, a breath of tune,
Nature's symphony beneath the moon.

The brooklet babbles, a gentle flow,
Its secrets shared with the rustling low.
Every stone glistens with tales untold,
In this enchanted grove of green and gold.

The branches arch like a painter's brush,
As twilight falls, the heartbeats hush.
Beneath the stars, the shadows blend,
In leafy realms where dreams ascend.

The roots entwined in a silent prance,
In sync with the rhythm of night's romance.
A melody woven in the cool night air,
Inviting all wanderers to linger there.

So heed the whispers, the soft-spun threads,
Of nature's lore where magic spreads.
In tidal rhythms, we find our place,
In the leafy realm, a warm embrace.

Cadence of Sylphs at Dusk

As day recedes with a tender sigh,
Sylphs flit about, as shadows fly.
In twilight's gleam, they weave and play,
A tapestry bright in the dusk's ballet.

With wings of argent, they dance so light,
Their laughter echoing through the night.
Each flicker a promise, a glimmer so rare,
In the cool evening air, magic fills the lair.

They twirl 'round the blossoms, so fragrant and sweet,
A cadence that pulses beneath our feet.
With whispers so soft, secrets they share,
Inviting the dreamers to join them there.

As stars emerge, their glow a guide,
The sylphs gather close, nature's pride.
They dance in circles, a wondrous sight,
An invitation to embrace the night.

In harmony with the nightingale's song,
They weave through the darkness, bright and strong.
The cadence of sylphs, a tale so bold,
In dusk's gentle arms, let dreams unfold.

Glimmers of Myth in the Forest's Heart

Deep in the wood where shadows play,
Glimmers of myth light the way.
In silvery beams, whispers collide,
Mysteries dance where secrets hide.

The ancient oaks stand tall and proud,
Guardians of magic, lost in the crowd.
With roots entwined like stories most rare,
They cradle the dreams drifting through air.

Elusive phantoms in twilight's grace,
With every step, a familiar face.
The heart of the forest beats strong and free,
In echoes of voices that call to thee.

Flickering lights in the underbrush,
Inviting the wanderers with gentle hush.
Each glimmer a tale waiting to unfold,
In the depths of the forest, mysteries told.

So tread softly on the leaf-strewn path,
Embrace the wonders found in its bath.
For glimmers of myth in the forest's heart,
Awaken the magic that sets us apart.

Sighs of Flora in the Evening Glow

As the sun bows low, the petals sigh,
In evening glow, their colors vie.
A tapestry woven of dusk's embrace,
Flora whispers softly, each touch a grace.

The daisies nod in the gentle breeze,
While willows sway with elegant ease.
In twilight's kiss, shadows dance near,
A soft serenade, the heart can hear.

The sky blushes pink with secrets shared,
While blooms exhale dreams, unprepared.
Each fragrant breath tells stories sweet,
Of sleepy gardens where fairies meet.

The twilight lingers, casting its spell,
As evening's slow curtain begins to swell.
Sighs of flora weave tales of the night,
In stars that descend, a delicate flight.

So linger a moment, let time unfold,
In the evening glow, where wonders are told.
For sighs of flora in twilight's embrace,
Invite all to wander in nature's grace.

Elysium in the Cradle of Pines

In the cradle of pines, where the moon does sigh,
Whispers of magic twinkle in the sky.
A veil of soft mist wraps the ancient trees,
Guarding secrets where the heart finds ease.

Stars wink playfully, casting silver light,
Over forest glens, where fairies take flight.
Each rustle of leaves tells a tale reborn,
In the enchanted night, where dreams are worn.

Crickets serenade in melodic tune,
While shadows dance gently beneath the moon.
Time flows like a river, calm and serene,
In this haven of wonders, forever unseen.

A flicker, a shimmer, as fireflies play,
Guiding lost wanderers who've lost their way.
Together they weave through the soft forest air,
In a world carved from whispers, free from despair.

Within the embrace of the pines so grand,
Lies a realm where wishes are close at hand.
In twilight's cocoon, let your spirit soar,
For Elysium whispers, beckoning for more.

Lush Labyrinths of Celestial Echoes

In lush labyrinths where mysteries dwell,
Celestial echoes cast their enchanting spell.
The paths intertwine, weaving tales untold,
Wrapped in a tapestry, both vibrant and bold.

Moonlight glimmers on petals of gold,
As secrets of ages begin to unfold.
Each twist of the journey sparks a new dream,
Flowing like a river, a silvery stream.

Laughter of nightingales fills the air,
With each fluttering wing, magic dances there.
Whispering winds share the stories of yore,
In lush labyrinths where the heart starts to soar.

The stars weave a canopy, celestial delight,
Painting every shadow with shimmering light.
Dance with the echoes of time long past,
In a serenade sung, forever to last.

In the embrace of the night, softly roam,
Among lush labyrinths, you will find home.
With each step you take, let your spirit sing,
For echoes of dreams are the treasures they bring.

Echoing Tales in the Ferny Hollows

In the ferny hollows where soft shadows creep,
Echoing tales of the forest, they keep.
A chorus of whispers weaves through the air,
In a haven of stories that linger with care.

Dappled sunlight glimmers through layers of green,
Illuminating secrets that once have been seen.
A flicker of movement, a rustle, a sigh,
Each tale that unfolds is a soft lullaby.

Moss carpets pathways, plush under foot,
Where ancient roots gather, steadfast and stoop.
Here, every heartbeat is part of the lore,
As nature's symphony echoes evermore.

With a sigh of the breeze, a new chapter's spun,
In ferny hollows where old tales are won.
The heart beats in rhythm with echoes of grace,
In these sacred spaces, you find your place.

So listen, dear wanderer, to the murmurs of fate,
In the ferny hollows, where stories await.
A tapestry woven of moments in time,
Echoing laughter, a sweet, silent rhyme.

Gleaming Chronicles of the Veiled Nymphs

In twilight's embrace, the veiled nymphs convene,
Gleaming chronicles hidden, yet seen.
Their laughter cascades like a babbling brook,
In moonlit glades, where magic is took.

With delicate grace, they dance in the night,
Weaving tales of enchantment, pure delight.
Their whispers enchant, filling hearts with song,
In their shimmering stories where spirits belong.

Petals unfurling in delicate bloom,
Reveal the soft light that banishes gloom.
Each memory penned in the ink of the stars,
Chronicles of wonder, unbound by the bars.

In the stillness of night, with the world held at bay,
The nymphs guide the dreamers who wander astray.
With each heartbeat, the forest does blend,
In gleaming chronicles where beginnings transcend.

So listen, dear dreamer, to the tales they weave,
Within starlit realms, in a midnight reprieve.
A dance of the nymphs, a story anew,
In the gleaming chronicles, your heart will ensue.

Serenade of the Twilight Glimmers

In twilight's soft and silken shroud,
The whispers weave a silver cloud,
Where shadows dance and laughter plays,
A symphony of dusky rays.

The moonlight pours like liquid dreams,
Upon the brook's soft, gentle gleams,
Where fireflies flit with whims so bright,
Enchanting hearts with pure delight.

Beneath the arch of ancient trees,
The rustling leaves sing melodies,
Each branch a note in nature's song,
A harmony that feels so strong.

The stars arise, their twinkling eyes,
Bear witness to the softest sighs,
Of creatures stirring in the night,
Awakening to newfound light.

In every nook, in every glade,
The twilight's charm shall never fade,
For in its depths, we find our place,
Embraced by night's enchanting grace.

Secrets Flitting Through the Sylvan Air

Beneath the boughs where secrets dwell,
The whispers of the forest swell,
With tales of old in breezes spun,
A dance of shadows, light, and fun.

The fae take flight on gossamer wings,
Their laughter echoes as it rings,
Through fragrant blooms and emerald glades,
Where every heartache swiftly fades.

Squirrels chatter, and the owls hoot,
While blooms unfold and roots take root,
In harmony with time's embrace,
Each nook adorned with nature's grace.

The sun dips low, and whispers grow,
As twilight casts its gentle glow,
Where shadows stitch the tales anew,
Of secrets shared by me and you.

So wander wide and listen keen,
For magic hides in sights unseen,
And every breeze that wraps the night,
Carries a song of pure delight.

Echoes of the Starlit Canopy

Beneath the vast and starlit dome,
The night reveals a hidden home,
Where echoes of the past reside,
In secret realms where dreams abide.

The cosmos hums a gentle tune,
As constellations shimmer and swoon,
With whispers of forgotten lore,
Awaiting hearts to seek and soar.

In twilight's grasp, the wonders gleam,
As time unfolds like woven seam,
Each twinkling star a silent sigh,
A gleaming dream that waves goodbye.

The nightingale weaves sweetness rare,
With notes that drift upon the air,
And every heart, when still and true,
Can hear the serenade anew.

So lie beneath the skies so wide,
And let the universe be your guide,
For in each echo, life's delight,
Awaits, aglow in starry night.

Melodies from the Faerie Realm

In glens where golden blossoms sway,
The faeries greet the break of day,
With laughter light as morning dew,
In fields of dreams where hopes come true.

A flicker here, a flutter there,
The magic hangs upon the air,
As melodies entwine in flight,
To paint the canvas of the night.

Their voices blend with rise and fall,
In harmony that weaves through all,
A song of joy, of love and care,
That dances with the sunlit flare.

Beneath the boughs of ancient trees,
The echoes drift upon the breeze,
Where every note brings peace and cheer,
And all our worries disappear.

So listen close, O heart so true,
To whispers wrapped in skies of blue,
For every faerie, every dream,
Crafts tales that shimmer and redeem.

Radiant Murmurs of the Forest

Beneath the boughs, the whispers rise,
In shadows deep where magic lies,
The woodland sings in soft refrain,
A lullaby of joy and pain.

The leaves dance lightly to the sound,
As ancient secrets all around,
With every rustle, truth unveils,
A tapestry of heart's details.

The brook chimes in with laughter bright,
Reflecting dreams that take to flight,
Each ripple speaks of tales untold,
Of courage fierce and hearts of gold.

When twilight falls, the fireflies gleam,
As if the stars forgot to dream,
They pulse and flicker, life anew,
In harmony, they weave the view.

The forest breathes, both wise and young,
In every note, a song is sung,
A symphony that binds us near,
In radiant murmurs, crystal clear.

Serenade of the Moonlit Canopy

Through branches arching, silver beams,
The night unfolds in lively dreams,
Each leaf adorned with glimmering light,
A serenade for the starry night.

The owls hoot softly, wisdom shared,
In shadows deep, their gaze is bared,
They guard the secrets dusk entwines,
In whispered breaths, the silence shines.

The wind, a melody so sweet,
Invites the heart to rise and beat,
As moonbeams trace the forest floor,
A canvas rich with tales of yore.

Beneath this canopy of dreams,
The nightingale in chorus seems,
To weave a spell of hope and grace,
A tender balm in nature's embrace.

With every note, the world aligns,
Like threads of fate in elegant designs,
The serenade of winds will guide,
Where magic sings, and love resides.

The Hidden Chorus of Nature

In verdant glades where shadows play,
A hidden chorus sings away,
Each creature's voice, a thread in time,
A symphony most pure, sublime.

The rustling leaves embrace the tone,
Each heartbeat echoes, not alone,
The crickets chirp in rhythmic cheer,
As blossoms sway, their joy sincere.

The buzzing bees hum songs of toil,
In fragrant blooms, they spin and coil,
While distant mountains softly speak,
The wisdom formed from valleys meek.

A delicate dance of night and day,
In harmony, they find their way,
The brook's soft gurgle, a lullaby,
That comforts all who wander by.

The hidden chorus, wild yet sweet,
Enlivens hearts with every beat,
In nature's arms, we find our place,
A timeless song, a warm embrace.

Gleams of Magic Through the Leaves

The sunlight spills like golden dreams,
Through emerald canopies, it beams,
Each glint a spark of ancient lore,
A dance of magic, evermore.

With every rustling wind that blows,
The whispers tell of what life knows,
In shadows deep, enchantments thrive,
Where dreams awaken, hearts revive.

The forest holds its secrets tight,
In fleeting glimpses of pure light,
A wink of fate through branches wild,
Reminding us, we're nature's child.

In every hue, a story wakes,
Each color whispers, life partakes,
Of wonders hidden from our gaze,
Yet ever-present in the haze.

As twilight cloaks the forest dim,
The gleams of magic on a whim,
Invite the spirit to believe,
In nature's art, we shall receive.

Flickering Echoes in the Glistening Dell

In the dell where whispers play,
Soft shadows dance, the light at bay.
Echoes flicker like fireflies,
Illuminating secrets and sighs.

A brook hums softly, tales unfold,
Of ancient woods and dreams untold.
Each leaf a witness to ages past,
Where moments linger, forever cast.

The moon hangs low, a silver thread,
Weaving stories of those who've fled.
A tapestry of mist and dreams,
Woven with hope and silver beams.

Footsteps soft on the carpet green,
As twilight flutters in between.
Flickering echoes scatter low,
Like memories dancing, aglow.

Beneath the stars, the secrets glow,
In the heart of woods where whispers flow.
In the glistening dell, magic thrives,
In flickering echoes, the past survives.

Carnival of Starlight in the Underbrush

In the underbrush where laughter sways,
A carnival of starlight plays.
Moonbeams twinkle like eyes aglow,
Under the canopy, shadows flow.

Fireflies gather, a shimmering fleet,
With each twirl, a rhythm sweet.
Leaves rustle soft, a gentle breeze,
Voices of night whisper with ease.

In every corner, magic blooms,
As flowers dance in the night's glooms.
Delight wraps round like a woven scarf,
In the heart of night, we laugh and laugh.

A jester moon rides high in the sky,
Painting the dark with a glittering sigh.
Beneath the branches, young hearts soar,
In starlit wonder, forevermore.

As dawn approaches, colors fade,
But the joy lingers, never betrayed.
In the underbrush, memories abide,
In a carnival of starlight, joy collide.

Secrets Stitched in Morning Dew

Morning dew glistens like precious lace,
Whispers of dawn in a tender embrace.
Each droplet holds a tale untold,
Secrets stitched in brilliance bold.

The world awakens with vibrant breath,
In the hush of morn, there lies no death.
Nature's canvas, fresh and new,
Painted with secrets in morning dew.

The petals yawn, stretch to pristine light,
Inviting the sun to the glorious sight.
A symphony played by dawn's gentle hand,
Telling the stories of this bright land.

Each blade of grass sings a soft hymn,
Of quiet moments, life not grim.
In the spark of dew, yesterday fades,
And new beginnings in stillness cascade.

Beneath the sky, the world is vast,
With secrets woven from shadows past.
In morning's hush, there's so much to view,
In the delicate dance of morning dew.

Life's Elysian Choreography Beneath the Trees

Beneath the trees, where echoes play,
Life twirls in a radiant ballet.
Branches sway to an ageless song,
As nature's whispers hum along.

Dappled sunlight filters through leaves,
With every rustle, the heart believes.
A graceful flurry, the world takes flight,
In the embrace of soft, golden light.

Each creature dances, in harmony found,
To the rhythm of life, profound.
The fawn leaps high, the owl takes flight,
In this choreography, pure delight.

With every step, a story unfolds,
In the tapestry of greens and golds.
Beneath the trees, where dreams intertwine,
Life's elysian waltz, so divine.

As twilight shades the vibrant gleam,
The forest whispers, a soothing dream.
In the stillness, the dance continues,
Beneath the trees, life's joy renews.

Hushed Utopias of Verdant Dreams

In the glen where shadows play,
Whispers weave the night away.
Dewdrops dance on leaves so bright,
Carving tales in silver light.

Swaying grasses hold the throng,
Chiming softly like a song.
Beneath the boughs, a secret home,
For lost souls who wander, roam.

Mossy banks and twilight air,
Mysteries linger everywhere.
Golden beams through branches stream,
Painting life in nature's dream.

Frogs croak songs of deep delight,
While fireflies take to the night.
In stillness lies a magic pure,
An ancient peace that will endure.

Hushed utopias softly sing,
Of the joys the wild will bring.
Embrace the wonders, let them gleam,
In heart and soul, let verdant dream.

Enlivened Echoes in the Mossy Hollow

Deep within the mossy vale,
Spirit voices weave a tale.
Rooted whispers call the stars,
Painting dreams with silver scars.

In the hollow where dreams nest,
Nature sings, a vibrant fest.
Each soft rustle, every breath,
Echoes life beyond the death.

Sunlight dapples through the leaves,
Where the gentle heart believes.
Ferns unfurl with tender grace,
In this verdant, sacred place.

Brambles weave their emerald lace,
While the brook finds its own pace.
Trickling songs of joy unfold,
Secrets in their ripples told.

Every heartbeat, every glance,
Invites nature's timeless dance.
Safe from time's eternal flow,
In Mossy Hollow, spirits glow.

Radiance of the Fey at Eventide

When the sun begins to wane,
And shadows stretch with soft refrain,
Fey lights flicker, glow, and gleam,
In the twilight's gentle dream.

Whispers twirl in evening air,
Spirits dart without a care.
Crystals shimmer in the light,
Stirring hearts to take their flight.

Petals sway with secrets near,
While the nightingale draws near.
In this realm of shimm'ring dawn,
Magic stirs and hearts are drawn.

Laughter dances 'neath the stars,
As the radiant fey play far.
Glimmers spark the leaves and loam,
In their warmth, we find our home.

So, behold the night unfold,
Tales of fey in whispers told.
In radiance, our dreams align,
With the magic that's divine.

Secrets of the Woodland Whispers

In the hush of towering pines,
Softly flow the hidden signs.
Nature's breath in gentle waves,
Secrets linger in the graves.

Twilight dances on the ground,
Through the trees, an ancient sound.
Murmurs echo, soft, profound,
Unraveling the world around.

Here, the fae and shadows twine,
Swaying subtly, intertwine.
In the air, a fragrance sweet,
Where the wild and wonder meet.

Every glance holds timeless charm,
Nature's spirit, ever warm.
Questions posed in twilight's grace,
Find their answer, face to face.

So, heed the whispers, soft and clear,
For the woodland tells us near.
In its secrets, lost and found,
Life's great wonders shall abound.

Shadows and Twinkles on Mossy Mounds

In the glade where moss does grow,
Shadows dance in soft moon glow.
Twinkling lights, like fireflies,
Guide the dreams, where magic lies.

Whispers float on evening air,
Tales of joy, of hope, and care.
Voices cradle nature's song,
Beneath the stars, we all belong.

Ancient trees with wisdom deep,
Guarding secrets that they keep.
Ferns and flowers softly sway,
Cradling night, welcoming day.

Footsteps light on earthen track,
Nature's call, there's no turning back.
With each breath, the world expands,
In this realm of thriving lands.

As dawn breaks, with gentle grace,
As shadows fade, we find our place.
Mossy mounds where wonders meet,
A kingdom vast beneath our feet.

Notes from Wistful Wings

In the hush of morning light,
Wings draw near, a graceful flight.
Songs from hearts that roam so free,
Carry whispers, just for thee.

With each flutter, tales unfold,
Of dreams pursued and secrets told.
Wistful wings in azure skies,
Brush the clouds, where freedom lies.

Every note's a gentle breeze,
Through the leaves of ancient trees.
Nature hums a soothing tune,
Underneath the watchful moon.

Across the fields, their tales unwind,
With every sweep, a bond we find.
Connecting souls in silent ways,
In the beauty of their grace.

Night will come, yet still they soar,
Echoes linger, wanting more.
Notes that crisscross, strong yet light,
Wistful wings, take flight tonight.

Celestial Ledger of Hidden Paths

In the night, the stars align,
Whispers chart the paths divine.
A celestial ledger unfolds,
With secrets only twilight holds.

Astrologers of old would speak,
Of destinies for hearts so meek.
Hidden paths traced by the light,
Guide the lost to find their sight.

Constellations weave a tale,
Of adventurers who prevail.
In the dark, the map ignites,
Leading souls to fateful nights.

Every star, a wish fulfilled,
Promises by starlit chill.
Navigation through cosmic streams,
Foretold in our deepest dreams.

Let us wander, hand in hand,
Through this vast and wondrous land.
Underneath the blanket bold,
Trails of starlight to behold.

Starlight Serenade from Stone to Stream

Underneath the silver sheen,
Where the stones meet valleys green.
A serenade begins to start,
As water sings, it flows like art.

Pebbles murmur, secrets shared,
In the night, the world is bared.
Rippling whispers, soft and clear,
Echoing songs for all to hear.

Starlight dances on the waves,
Carving paths through moonlit caves.
Each reflection tells a tale,
Of journeys where the heart sets sail.

Every note is nature's breath,
In this symphony of life and death.
From the rock to gentle stream,
Weaving wonders like a dream.

So let us pause and feel the sound,
In these waters, magic's found.
A starlit serenade we trust,
In flowing peace, we find our rust.

Hushed Reflections in the Brooding Twilight

In twilight's grasp, the shadows creep,
As whispers float through silence deep.
A gentle breeze with secrets shares,
With tales of dreams and hidden cares.

The moon ascends, its silver glow,
Illuminates the tales we know.
With every sigh, the stars align,
In brooding depths, the night is fine.

Each fleeting thought, a fragile spark,
Resides within the velvet dark.
Reflections dance like shadows cast,
In twilight's arms, the moments last.

The heartbeats echo, soft and low,
As time entwines in ebb and flow.
A symphony of sighs and dreams,
Where memories linger in moonbeams.

Embrace the night, let worries cease,
Find solace in the dusk's release.
For in this hush, a truth resides,
In every star, our hope abides.

Whimsical Footfalls in the Secret Wood

Beneath the boughs where secrets thrive,
The whispers of the woods come alive.
Footfalls dance on mossy ground,
In tangled paths where faeries abound.

Every rustle, a tale to unveil,
Of ancient magic, gentle and frail.
With every step, enchantments flow,
In the heart of the wood, all will glow.

Sunbeams flicker through leafy seams,
Weaving light into vivid dreams.
A melody of life entwined,
In each shadow, new wonders find.

The wildflowers sway in playful cheer,
While whispers of secrets drift near.
In this haven, hearts can soar,
In the magic of a woodland lore.

So follow the path where stories bloom,
Where sprites and wonders chase the gloom.
In whimsical footfalls, joy unfolds,
In the secret wood, where life beholds.

Charmed Soundtrack of the Elunarian Forest

In the Elunarian Forest, music weaves,
Through golden leaves and ancient eaves.
A harp of wind strums soft and low,
While melodies in twilight flow.

Each rustling branch a note complete,
Where echoes dance on phantom feet.
The symphony of night takes flight,
In harmony with stars so bright.

Elves entwine with nature's grace,
Each tune a spell in this sacred space.
With laughter and song, enchantments blend,
Painting the dusk as day must end.

The brook hums softly, a lullaby,
While fireflies twinkle, a fleeting sigh.
In every chord, a story glows,
The forest's heart in music flows.

So listen close to the whispers near,
For every note holds magic dear.
Where silence fades in symphonic dream,
In Elunarian woods, life's a gleam.

Pastoral Enchantment of Picturesque Memories

In fields where golden sunsets lie,
The pastoral charm invites a sigh.
With echoes soft of laughter spun,
In picturesque moments, joys begun.

The meadows bloom with colors bright,
A tapestry woven in tender light.
Each breeze a whisper of days gone by,
As time drifts gently, like clouds on high.

Children's laughter, pure and free,
Dances with shadows of yesteryear's glee.
In every glance, a treasure found,
In nostalgic dreams, softly profound.

The twilight calls, with hues so warm,
Wrapped in nature's enchanting form.
From past to present, the heart can see,
The beauty of life, in memory's glee.

So hold the moments as seasons blend,
In pastoral dreams that never end.
For in each heartbeat, life's song remains,
In picturesque memories, love sustains.

Lullabies of the Phantom Brush

In the stillness of the night,
Soft whispers cradle the air,
An artist's hand, with gentle light,
Paints dreams beyond compare.

Echoes twirl on velvet skies,
Each stroke a tale unspun,
Where shadows dance and shadows rise,
And twilight's song has begun.

Moonlit beams caress the creek,
Where secrets weave in silken thread,
The brush, it murmurs, tender, weak,
A lullaby for dreams unfed.

As stars unlace their shimmering gems,
The forest breathes a sigh,
In the distance, softly hems,
The magic never dies.

So rest your heart, let worries cease,
Let colors blend and swirl,
In the arms of night, find peace,
And in dreams, let love unfurl.

Harmonies of Sylvan Light

In wooded realm where shadows play,
The sunbeams thread with grace,
They weave a tune, both bright and gay,
In nature's sweet embrace.

The whispers of the leaves in sway,
Compose a song so pure,
The breezes, gentle, softly play,
A harmony to endure.

Amidst the trunks, old stories sigh,
Of creatures wise and bold,
They dance beneath the endless sky,
In melodies untold.

The flowers nod in vibrant hues,
Their petals form a choir,
The world, adorned in sparkles, views,
The symphony of fire.

So listen close, let spirits rise,
Feel nature's heart so bright,
In sylvan bounds, where beauty lies,
Embrace the endless light.

Twilight's Ethereal Tweak of the Heart

When twilight spills its pastel hues,
And thoughts begin to blend,
A softness like a whispered muse,
Where dreams and daylight mend.

The whispers of the setting sun,
Tug gently at the soul,
With each breath, a journey begun,
As shadows start to roll.

In fading warmth, the heart will sway,
To rhythms of the dusk,
As starlit paths light up the way,
And love's sweet breath is hushed.

With every glowing star that gleams,
A promise woven tight,
In twilight's glow, we chase our dreams,
As whispers fill the night.

So close your eyes and drift away,
Let heartstrings softly part,
In twilight's grace, forever stay,
Embracing every heart.

Whispers in the Woods of Loneliness

In the tangled woods, a silence reigns,
A chill that clings like dew,
Each whisper echoes, soft remains,
Of dreams that once we knew.

The trees, they lean with heavy sighs,
Their branches softly groan,
As shadows stretch with longing eyes,
To seek what's left alone.

The paths are worn with tales untold,
Each step a heavy heart,
Where echoes of the brave and bold,
Finish before they start.

In the twilight, feelings freeze,
And loneliness takes flight,
Yet still the wind through boughs will tease,
A flicker of the light.

So dare to tread where silence sleeps,
For in the woods, we find,
Though shadows cloak our hidden griefs,
There's solace in the mind.

Erewhon's Melody in Rustling Tresses

In the glen where whispers weave,
The echoes of forgotten tales,
Beneath the boughs, the old trees grieve,
For secrets lost in soft night gales.

The moonlight dances, silver bright,
Casting shadows on the cool ground,
As fireflies twinkle in their flight,
In harmony, a magic sound.

Each breeze carries a gentle sigh,
Where dreams are spun with golden thread,
In silken hues, the night draws nigh,
To cradle hopes and dreams long shed.

Through rustling leaves, in soft repose,
The world unveils its whispered grace,
A symphony of highs and lows,
In nature's warm, embracing space.

Here under stars, where wonders spark,
The heart finds peace in gentle night,
As Erewhon's song ignites the dark,
And fills the soul with sweet delight.

Musings of the Glistening Brook

Along the banks where waters flow,
The brook hums soft, a tranquil tune,
With pebbles round, a gentle show,
Reflecting light beneath the moon.

It sings of journeys, far and wide,
Of hidden paths and trails anew,
As breezes dance, the currents glide,
In rippling dreams, the heart breaks through.

Each drop a treasure, pure and clear,
It tells of laughter, joy, and pain,
From distant lands it brings us near,
In whispers sweet as summer rain.

The silvered dance of shadows play,
Where nature's brush strokes life so bright,
In every ripple, night meets day,
And time, a fleeting spark of light.

Here by the brook, the soul can rest,
In thought, in peace, just being free,
It cradles me, a gentle nest,
In nature's arms, my heart finds glee.

Tapestry of Light in the Hushed Glade

In the glade where silence reigns,
The light weaves through the ancient trees,
A tapestry with golden veins,
As whispers float upon the breeze.

Each ray a hope, each shadow a sigh,
As sunbeams dance on emerald leaves,
In quietude, where spirits fly,
The heart, in reverie, believes.

Amidst the blooms, in softest hue,
Petals unfurl to greet the dawn,
Each moment felt, a gift so true,
In nature's arms, I feel reborn.

The hush enfolds like velvet night,
As stars emerge, a twinkling stream,
And in that glow, all feels just right,
As dreams entwine in waking dream.

In every crease of light that falls,
A story shared, a life unveiled,
In the glade, where wonder calls,
A sacred peace, eternally hailed.

Ethereal Soliloquy of the Wildflowers

In fields where wildflowers bloom so bright,
An ethereal voice begins to sing,
In colors bursting, pure delight,
Each petal tells of spring's offering.

With whispers soft, the blossoms sway,
In gentle rhythm with the breeze,
A soliloquy that finds its way,
Through rustling grass and ancient trees.

They paint the earth in vibrant hues,
A canvas made of nature's grace,
In every shade, the morning muse,
Finds solace in this sacred space.

As bees hum out their busy song,
And sunlight warms the life around,
The wildflowers, bold and strong,
Gather dreams from seeds unbound.

In twilight's glow, they take their rest,
These fragile souls of beauty's best,
A tapestry of life expressed,
In nature's heart, they are the quest.

Harmonies of the Fey

In glades where twilight dances free,
The whispering winds hum soft and low,
A harmony of petals, wild and glee,
Unraveled is the night's sweet glow.

Beneath the arching, starlit trees,
Echoes of laughter weave through air,
Each note a secret, carried with ease,
A melody beyond compare.

With every breeze, the shadows sway,
As moonbeams stitch the dreams anew,
With every dream, the fairies play,
In realms where magic always grew.

The flowers nod and songbirds trace,
The paths where ancient tales abide,
In moments stitched with time and grace,
The Fey reveal their hidden side.

So wander here, where magic sings,
And let your heart converse with light,
For in this realm where beauty clings,
The Harmonies of Fey take flight.

Lullabies from the Misty Vale

In shadows soft, the whispers weave,
A lullaby of twilight's songs,
Where ancient trees and dreams believe,
And in their roots, the magic throngs.

With silver streams that gently wend,
Through mossy stones in emerald hues,
Each note, a promise, never to end,
Cradled in night's embrace, it grew.

The mist rolls in, a tender shroud,
Embracing moments lost in time,
A symphony for every crowd,
In harmony, the fey bells chime.

So close your eyes, feel peace descend,
As lullabies from vale call near,
With every breath, let fears unbend,
And drift away on dreams sincere.

In the Misty Vale, where soft lights glow,
The secrets of the night unfold,
In songs of love, the spirits flow,
A tale of wonder, softly told.

Tones of the Enchanted Realm

Beyond the ridge where wonders gleam,
The tones of magic swirl and play,
Each note a spark, a vibrant dream,
In the enchanted realm, we sway.

From bubbling brooks to drooping boughs,
Where twilight weaves her purple threads,
Every whisper to the moon allows,
A tranquil heart where magic spreads.

In colors bold and shadows light,
With every sigh, the echoes flow,
The universe ignites the night,
In echoing tune, we come to know.

With every twist, the flowers bloom,
Their petals dance to nature's song,
Embraced by joy, dispelling gloom,
Where all enchanted souls belong.

So tread this path of sweetest sounds,
Let music guide your heart's delight,
For in the realm where love abounds,
The tones of magic set us right.

The Dance of Shimmering Spirits

In moonlit glades where shadows twirl,
The spirits dance with gleaming grace,
Their laughter weaves a silken whirl,
As stars alight, embrace the space.

With every spin, a story flows,
Of magic spun from dreams long past,
In shimmering hues, the mystery grows,
Their gentle whisper holds us fast.

In breezes soft, they shake and sway,
The colors swirl in a sweet trance,
Where echoes of the night betray,
The secrets held in each bright glance.

So let us join their fleeting flight,
To dance with spirits, wild and free,
In harmony with the starry night,
We'll waltz 'neath ancient, trembling trees.

For in this realm, where dreams collide,
And every heart learns how to sing,
The Dance of Spirits shall abide,
With joy that only magic brings.

Resonance of the Evergreen

In whispers soft, the trees will sway,
Their emerald crowns in gentle play.
Through branches high, the breezes speak,
Of ancient tales that nature seeks.

Among the roots, where shadows dwell,
The secrets linger, weave a spell.
With every rustle, life takes flight,
In harmony with day and night.

The woodland's heart, a sacred space,
Embracing all in warm embrace.
Through tangled paths, the stories flow,
Of whispered dreams, where mortals go.

Glimmers of hope in every thrum,
A symphony of life's soft hum.
As sunlight filters through the boughs,
The forest breathes, and time allows.

So heed the call, the verdant call,
Within the woods, we are but small.
Yet in their arms, we find our way,
Resonance bright, come what may.

Echoing Secrets of the Sylphs

In twilight's glow, the sylphs do dance,
With gossamer wings, they weave romance.
They flit and flutter, elusive, free,
Guardians of secrets, wild as the sea.

In sighs of wind, their laughter rings,
Through flowers blooming, on ethereal wings.
They whisper magic in the starlit night,
With each soft echo, they ignite delight.

Beneath the moon, where shadows play,
The sylphs twirl in a merry ballet.
Their voices weave a spell so sweet,
Drawn from the dreams where worlds do meet.

A tapestry spun from stardust and air,
In every rustling leaf, a love affair.
They guide the lost on paths unknown,
In every shadow, their magic is shown.

So listen close, let your heart take flight,
In the sylphs' embrace, they light the night.
For in their laughter, the world awakes,
Echoing secrets, as the dawn breaks.

Rhapsody of the Luminous Glade

In a glade where the moonlight meets,
A rhapsody hums in soft heartbeats.
With every leaf, a story sings,
Of shimmering nights and wondrous things.

The fireflies dance like scattered stars,
A galaxy clipped by gentle jars.
With every flicker, a message flows,
In this place where the night wind blows.

The luminescent blooms begin to sway,
As if to greet the end of day.
Their colors twinkle in dusky light,
A painter's dream, a pure delight.

In whispered tones, the shadows weave,
A melody that does not leave.
It carries hopes on silken threads,
As dreams are born on twilight's beds.

So wander here, where magic lies,
Beneath the glow of endless skies.
In the luminous glade, where spirits soar,
The rhapsody calls, forevermore.

Fables of the Woven Light

In ancient woods, where light is spun,
Each fable whispered, a tale begun.
The threads of gold and silver gleam,
Weaving wisdom in every dream.

Amidst the boughs, the stories rise,
Dancing softly, like autumn sighs.
With tales of courage, love, and plight,
They bloom like stars in endless night.

Through misty paths, the echoes tread,
Of laughter, tears, in silence said.
For every heart that yearns to know,
The woven light will guide and show.

By starry skies and whispered stream,
These fables whisper in twilight's beam.
Embrace the tales of old and new,
In woven light, find strength anew.

So gather close, let shadows fade,
In fables spun, our souls are laid.
With every heart, the light ignites,
In magic's glow, our true paths write.

Carols Beneath the Ancient Boughs

Beneath the boughs, where whispers dwell,
The carols rise, like a casting spell.
Moonlight dances with a silver grace,
In this enchanted, timeless space.

Leaves sway gently, in the night's embrace,
Each note a memory, a soft trace.
The melody weaves through shadows deep,
Awakening dreams from their slumbering sleep.

Voices echo from the forest's heart,
With every strum, a hidden art.
In the stillness, the magic calls,
A symphony beneath the ancient walls.

Stars align in a celestial choir,
As if the heavens conspire.
Together they sing of tales untold,
Of joy, of wonder, and love of old.

So gather 'round, in the soft moonlight,
Embrace the songs of the wondrous night.
For in this moment, all fears release,
Under the branches, we find our peace.

Melodies of Twilight Whispers

As twilight falls, the whispers soar,
Echoes linger on the evening's shore.
A melody born from the dusk so fine,
Cradled softly, like vintage wine.

The stars awaken, one by one,
Painting stories of solace and fun.
Gentle breezes carry each refrain,
In stillness, we find joy amid pain.

With every note, the shadows sway,
In the dance of night, they find their way.
Harmony wraps around the trees,
Whispering secrets on the autumn breeze.

Night will weave its cloaks of charm,
Embracing hearts, enveloping warm.
These melodies paint the sky in gold,
A tapestry where dreams unfold.

So pause a while and close your eyes,
Let twilight's song be your guiding skies.
For in these whispers, hope rekindles,
In melodies born, the spirit kindles.

The Allure of the Hidden Path

Deep in the woods, where shadows blend,
Lies a hidden path that twists and bends.
With every step, enchantments sigh,
Inviting wanderers to draw nigh.

Whispers beckon through the leafy veil,
In the air, the scent of an ancient tale.
Secrets linger in the evening glow,
On this verdant trail, where few dare go.

Footprints fade, yet spirits remain,
In every nook, a soft refrain.
The allure calls with a gentle gaze,
Through tangled branches, in a mystic haze.

A brook's laughter dances near,
Echoing dreams, both bold and clear.
Each curve reveals a world anew,
Where magic dances, and visions accrue.

Journey forth, let your heart be free,
In the embrace of the ancient tree.
For within the woods, where whispers last,
Lies the allure of the hidden past.

Cacophony of Star-kissed Shadows

In the dark, where shadows prance,
A cacophony of night takes its chance.
Stars wink brightly in the velvet sky,
While ghosts of dreams in silence fly.

The wind will croon an untold song,
As the echoes of night dance along.
With every rustle, stories unfold,
In this arena, daring and bold.

Moonlight glimmers on murmuring streams,
Reflecting the essence of hidden dreams.
Each gurgle and sigh, a tale to share,
Cascading secrets on the midnight air.

A symphony born from the heart of night,
Where shadows mingle, a wondrous sight.
Let the clamor of stars guide your way,
As shadows embrace the end of day.

So listen close, to the starry tune,
In the nighttime's arms, beneath the moon.
For in this cacophony, hearts take flight,
Bound together in the magic of night.

Whispers in the Glade

Beneath the boughs where secrets sleep,
The softest words begin to creep,
In twilight's breath, the shadows swirl,
A dance of light, a dream unfurl.

The mossy floor, a tapestry,
Of ancient lore and mystery,
With every rustle, every sigh,
The whispers float, as time goes by.

A silver brook, its laughter near,
Reflects the stars, both bright and clear,
The trees stand tall, their stories bold,
In every ring, a tale retold.

In twilight's hush, the glade awakes,
As silver-eyed the night partakes,
Of dreams we weave and hearts that yearn,
In hidden paths, the lanterns burn.

The moon-kissed leaves, they softly sway,
In gentle tunes, the night will play,
A symphony of dark and light,
In whispers soft, the magic's sight.

Murmurs of the Woodland

In the heart of the woodlands, wild and free,
A tapestry of life sings quietly,
Branches entwine, the breath of trees,
Murmurs rise soft, like a summer breeze.

Dappled sunlight plays on the ground,
Footsteps echo where dreams are found,
With each rustle, a tale unfolds,
In the warmth of the earth, the magic behold.

The creatures dart, with glances shy,
In playful games, they leap and sigh,
Each murmur intertwines, as if to say,
In the woodland's heart, we find our way.

The flowers bloom in shades of light,
Their colors dance under the moonlit night,
With petals soft, they share their grace,
In whispered tones, they find their place.

A symphony of life in the trees above,
In the woodland's heart, we find our love,
In every note, the soul does ignite,
As murmurs blend with the gentle night.

Shadows of Laughter and Light

In a realm where shadows play their games,
Laughter echoes, calling out names,
The dance of dusk, a fleeting delight,
With every flicker, we chase the night.

Moonbeams stretch like fingers bright,
Grasping dreams in the soft twilight,
The forest's joy, a radiant sound,
In every glade, adventure found.

Where laughter mingles with whispered lore,
The trickster spirits beg for more,
In shadows cast by an ancient tree,
The tales of old come rushing free.

Beyond the veil where secrets lay,
The laughter weaves through night and day,
With every echo, the world ignites,
In shadows bare, there shines the light.

In the fabric of time, we weave our dreams,
Beneath the stars, our laughter beams,
For in this dance of shadows bright,
We find our joy, our hearts take flight.

Secrets in the Thicket

Amidst the thorns, where whispers wait,
Secrets linger, sealed by fate,
In tangled roots, the mysteries grow,
In hushed tones, the ancients know.

Every path, a story hides,
In the heart of the thicket, truth abides,
With softest breath, the leaves confide,
In echoes sweet, the dreams reside.

The twilight glimmers, a twinkling spark,
As creatures stir within the dark,
With cautious steps, they roam and peer,
To find the light, to quell the fear.

A fluttering heart in shadows deep,
Nestled secrets, the woods do keep,
For in this thicket, magic flows,
In every rustle, the mystery grows.

So seek the truth where few dare roam,
In thickets wild, we find our home,
With every step in nature's throng,
We weave the threads of life's sweet song.

Crescendo of the Moonlit Thicket

In the heart of night, where shadows creep,
Whispers of secrets in silence steep.
Branches sway gently, in a dance so light,
Awakening creatures that thrive out of sight.

The silver moon casts a gentle gleam,
Over paths where lost souls dare to dream.
Each rustling leaf tells a story so bold,
Of magic and wonder, in whispers retold.

Stars twinkle bright in the velvet dome,
Guiding the wanderers far from home.
Echoes of laughter blend with the breeze,
Carrying wishes, like ghosts through the trees.

Time seems to halt; the world holds its breath,
As nature conjures the spell of life and death.
A crescendo rises, a melody sweet,
In the moonlit thicket, where heartbeats meet.

With each passing moment, the night takes flight,
In the symphony woven of darkness and light.
Under the watchful gaze of the moon's soft glow,
The thicket sings softly, where all secrets flow.

Pamela's Flickering Lanterns

Pamela dances with lanterns aglow,
Her laughter, like echoes, in twilight's flow.
Beneath arching boughs, they twinkle and sway,
Guiding lost travelers along their dark way.

Each lantern a beacon, a flickering flame,
Casting soft shadows, embracing her name.
With whispers of hope caught in fragrant air,
She leads them to places where dreams dare to share.

The night holds a magic that none can resist,
In the glow of her lanterns, the mists softly twist.
She weaves through the woodland, a sprite full of grace,
Illuminating paths in this hidden place.

Adventurers gather, their spirits alight,
Beneath Pamela's lanterns, in the deep of the night.
Stories unfold like petals in bloom,
Each moment a treasure, dispelling the gloom.

Her dance is a promise, a gift wrapped in gold,
In the flickering light, the brave hearts grow bold.
Through shadows they wander, where mysteries chime,
Entranced by the lanterns, they dance out of time.

Spellbound Crickets' Midnight Symphony

At midnight's embrace, the crickets arise,
Their song a spell woven under moonlit skies.
Chirps and whispers blend, a delicate tune,
Inviting the night to dance 'neath the moon.

With each note they play, the world breathes anew,
A concert of shadows in indigo hue.
Leaves rustle softly, in rhythm with sound,
As nature rejoices, enchantment profound.

Stars shimmer brightly, like jewels on a crown,
Observing the crickets as darkness falls down.
They cradle the magic in melodies clear,
Drawing forth wonders that only they hear.

The symphony swells; the magic ignites,
In the heart of the night, where the world feels so right.
Each chirp holds a promise, a wish spun with care,
In the hush of the twilight, dreams flutter in air.

As dawn's fingers stretch and the first light begins,
The crickets grow quiet, their symphony thins.
Yet the echoes remain in the heart's silent space,
Of a night spent in wonder, in nature's embrace.

Dreams Carried by the Wind

When the night is still, and the world bows low,
Dreams take to the sky, as soft breezes blow.
They flutter like petals, on a journey unseen,
Whispering secrets of what might have been.

Carried away on the wings of the night,
Hopes dance like fireflies, glowing so bright.
Each wish that is floated on soft violet streams,
Unfolds like a story, alive in our dreams.

Through valleys and hills, they wander so free,
Tracing the lines of our hopes and our glee.
Like sails on the sea, they ride on the gust,
In the heart of the night, they shimmer with trust.

As dawn starts to rise, a golden embrace,
The wind hums a tune of a warm, gentle grace.
With each passing moment, new dreams come to play,
In the cradle of morning, the night fades away.

Yet echoes remain, in our hearts they reside,
The dreams carried forth, where our fancies abide.
In the soft light of morning, let us hold tight,
To the whispers of dreams that took flight in the night.

Twilight's Embrace Around the Gnarled Roots

In twilight's glow, shadows bend low,
Where roots entwine, as whispers flow.
Stars blink awake, in velvet hue,
While secrets linger, old yet new.

Moss carpets paths where dreams can tread,
An ancient song, by moonlight led.
Boughs cradle tales of love and woe,
As time drifts softly, like falling snow.

The air is thick with magic's breath,
In every nook that life bequeaths.
With each soft rustle, stories weave,
Of things unseen, that we believe.

Figures dance in a silvery beam,
The forest pulses, alive with dream.
Golden eyes blink in tender night,
With twinkling lights that shimmer bright.

So linger here, let heartstrings tug,
In twilight's arms, feel the warm hug.
For in the roots, where shadows play,
Magic lingers, to gently sway.

Phantoms of the Woodland Air

Among the trees where whispers sigh,
Phantoms of old, beneath the sky.
A light breeze carries tales of yore,
Inviting hearts to seek the lore.

With delicate grace, leaves flutter near,
Like spirits drawing ever near.
Footfalls echo on paths unseen,
Where memories fade but spirits glean.

The moon hangs low, a watchful eye,
Upon the dreams that softly fly.
In the hush before the dawn's embrace,
A fleeting moment in time and space.

Ghostly laughter twirls on the air,
A melody sweet, a soft, sweet care.
Lost in the mist, they dance and sway,
Warding off the light of day.

So linger on this twilight trail,
Where shadows whisper, and secrets sail.
In woodland's heart, let dreams take flight,
And find your home in starry night.

Whirlwinds of Pixie Laughter

In a glade where the wildflowers bloom,
Pixies gather, chasing the gloom.
With laughter that sparkles like morning dew,
Winding tales of mischief anew.

They whirl in circles, a dazzling sight,
Painting the air with joyful light.
Each fluttering wing, a flurry of glee,
Carving their secrets in each leafy spree.

Beneath the boughs where shadows dance,
They weave enchantments in a fleeting glance.
With twinkling eyes and mischief aglow,
They play in the shadows where no one can go.

Oh, join the revel, let laughter soar,
In whirlwinds that beckon and hearts that explore.
For in this magic, let troubles cease,
As pixies gather to bring sweet peace.

So tiptoe lightly on the earth's embrace,
Find the pathway where joy leaves no trace.
For within these woods, their laughter still sings,
A melody sweet that forever clings.

Veiled Secrets Among the Ferns

Amidst the ferns, a shrouded light,
Where whispers of ancient wisdom ignite.
Roots weave stories of those who roam,
Echoes of lives that found a home.

Beneath each frond, a secret stirs,
With rustling tales of forgotten furs.
A dance of shadows, a flicker of leaves,
Where nature cradles all it weaves.

In the heart of dusk, the colors blend,
As twilight dances, shadows bend.
With every rustle, a promise to share,
The veiled secrets of the woodland air.

So gather close, let stories unfold,
Of magic and wonder, worth more than gold.
For in every frond, and every sigh,
Lies the beauty of what never dies.

Let the forest wrap you in its care,
With gentle whispers, along the air.
For among the ferns, the heart can see,
The veiled secrets that set us free.